y

C. 1

ART PROFILES
For Kids
REMBRANDT

P.O. Box 196
Hockessin, Delaware 19707
Visit us on the web: www.mitchelllane.com
Comments? email us: mitchelllane@mitchelllane.com

ART PROFILES FOR KIDS

Titles in the Series

Art Profiles
For Kids
REMBRANDT

Russell Roberts

Mitchell Lane
PUBLISHERS

P.O. Box 196
Hockessin, Delaware 19707
Visit us on the web: www.mitchelllane.com
Comments? email us: mitchelllane@mitchelllane.com

Printing   1   2   3   4   5   6   7   8   9

Library of Congress Cataloging-in-Publication Data
Roberts, Russell, 1953-
   Rembrandt / by Russell Roberts.
      p. cm.—(Art profiles for kids)
   Includes bibliographical references and index.
   ISBN 978-1-58415-710-6 (library bound)
   1. Rembrandt Harmenszoon van Rijn, 1606-1669—Juvenile literature. 2. Artists—Netherlands—Biography—Juvenile literature. I. Rembrandt Harmenszoon van Rijn, 1606-1669. II. Title.
N6953.R4R63 2009
759.9492—dc22
[B]
                                                                                        2008002241

ABOUT THE AUTHOR: Russell Roberts has written and published nearly 40 books for adults and children on a variety of subjects, including baseball, memory power, business, New Jersey history, and travel. He has written numerous books for Mitchell Lane Publishers, including *Nathaniel Hawthorne, Thomas Jefferson, Holidays and Celebrations in Colonial America, Daniel Boone, The Lost Continent of Atlantis, Nostradamus,* and *Athena.* He lives in Bordentown, New Jersey, with his family and a fat, fuzzy, and crafty calico cat named Rusti.

ABOUT THE COVER: The images on the cover are paintings by the various artists in this series.

PHOTO CREDITS: pp. 9, 25, 40—Jupiter Images; p. 11—painting by Johannes Vermeer; p. 17—painting by Gerrit Adriaenszoon Berckheyde; p. 33—painting by Peter Paul Rubens; all other artwork by Rembrandt.

PUBLISHER'S NOTE: The facts on which this story is based have been thoroughly researched. Documentation of such research appears on page 47. While every possible effort has been made to ensure accuracy, the publisher will not assume liability for damages caused by inaccuracies in the data, and makes no warranty on the accuracy of the information contained herein.

PLB

Table of Contents

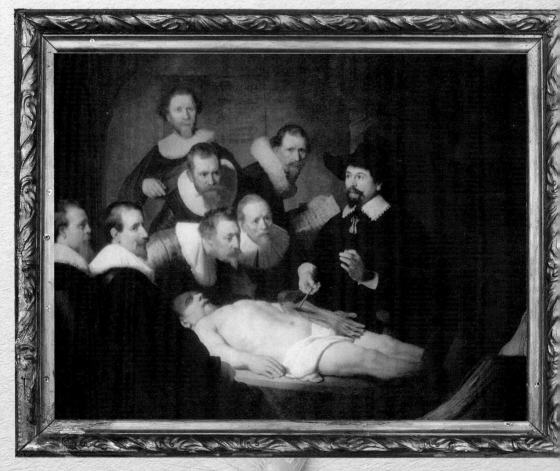

The Anatomy Lesson of Dr. Nicolaes Tulp was a great success for young Rembrandt, setting a new standard of excellence for group portraits. Rembrandt charged the painting with tension and excitement, which was much different from the stiff, formal group portraits common in the 1640s.

one

The Masterpiece

The artist stood before the canvas, a paintbrush in his fingers and concentration deeply etched on his brow. Occasionally he wet the brush with fresh paint, stepped forward, and made a few strokes on the canvas. Then he stepped back and stared at the picture. He was studying the artwork in front of him, but try as he might, he could not prevent other images from entering his mind. They were not happy ones.

One day this man, Rembrandt Harmenszoon van Rijn, would be recognized as one of the world's best artists of all time. His skill would be so highly regarded that his name would become synonymous with the pinnacle of a profession—in other words, a person could be "the Rembrandt" of one's trade.

That day in 1642, however, Rembrandt was a respected artist in the city of Amsterdam, but he was not considered the greatest in history. He had made his name painting portraits of prosperous Dutch citizens, for this was the country's Golden Age. The Netherlands was one of the richest and most powerful countries in the world, and one way the citizens displayed this wealth was by having their portraits painted. It is possible that today we know more about their appearance and their society than that of any other people in history before the camera was invented.[1]

As Rembrandt stood at his easel, he was working on a type of artwork that the Dutch had uniquely conceived—the group portrait.[2] This was a painting of a group of people, such as a company of soldiers or a body of government leaders, who commissioned an artist to paint them. Each person in the painting paid a portion of the artist's fee. Each expected to be

prominently featured. Usually the final product looked as if all the people were posing, because the artist tried to make everyone look important. This made it hard to inject any sense of realism into the work. Such group portraits as *The Anatomy Lesson of Dr. Sebastiaen Egbertsz* by Amsterdam artist Thomas de Keyser were stiff, formal, and posed, despite de Keyser's best efforts.

When he was younger, Rembrandt had broken that mold and scored a major success in group portraits. Soon after he came to Amsterdam he had produced the electrifying *The Anatomy Lesson of Dr. Nicolaes Tulp,* a masterful work that shows all of the characters in nervous motion. The huge painting is so realistic, it seems some of the people in it are about to come to life and speak. Rembrandt was only twenty-six when he painted it.

Now the older Rembrandt toiled on a new group portrait. As he painted it would be understandable if he had reflected on his early years. Back then he had been a youth newly arrived in Amsterdam, and *Dr. Tulp* had acted like a calling card, announcing this brilliant new artist. Soon after that he had met and married the lovely Saskia. How happy the two of them had been in their first years of marriage! He had painted his wife in a variety of beautiful costumes and poses. Once he had painted the two of them at a banquet, he holding a glass of beer aloft with a broad smile on his face, and she sitting coyly on his lap. They were young, happy, prosperous, and carefree.

All too soon Saskia had begun a long decline due to illness. Then came their infant children, dead just months after birth. Never careful with money, Rembrandt had spent, spent, and spent some more. His finances had steadily eroded.

Within the past few years had come the heaviest blows of all. First his mother, then his beloved Saskia, had died. The large house Rembrandt had bought for his wife must have seemed empty and quiet.

Sometimes out of intense personal pain, a great artist can rise up and create something extraordinary, and that is exactly what Rembrandt was accomplishing. The group portrait he was creating, now popularly known as *The Night Watch* but originally titled *The Company of Captain Frans Banning Cocq and Lieutenant Willem van Ruytenburgh,* is considered his masterpiece.

The Company of Captain Frans Banning Cocq and Lieutenant Willem van Ruytenburgh is considered by many to be Rembrandt's masterpiece. The popular title *The Night Watch* was given to it in later years, after too much varnish was placed on it in an effort to protect it. The varnish darkened it instead.

The painting depicts an Amsterdam militia company. By the 1640s, militia companies were no longer required to defend Amsterdam, and had become mere social groups.[3] Instead of showing the men sitting at a table or standing stiffly at attention, Rembrandt charged the scene with action. The portrait shows a group that does not seem quite ready to march into battle. In the center the captain and lieutenant are starting off, but in the background other members of the company look confused and uncertain of how to proceed. Some are raising weapons, others are examining or loading muskets, and others beat drums or unfurl flags.

The confusion of the scene is further emphasized by the figures that are shown trapped in the midst of this sudden action. In the corner a dog barks at a drummer, while in the center is a worried-looking young girl in a white dress (does she resemble Saskia?[4]) with a bird tied to her belt. She has apparently wandered into a scene that has sprung to terrifying life around her.

What makes the painting more than just a realistic view of men playing soldiers is the brilliant use of light—a Rembrandt trademark. Not only does he use light to emphasize certain characters in the painting, but he also uses it to balance the portrait. The little girl in the white dress, for instance, helps to counterbalance one of the figures in a yellow uniform, who otherwise would dominate the painting. Some figures are lit more than others, but while the eye is initially drawn to the lighter figures, it eventually seeks out those who are dimmer.

There is more—much more—to the painting, but for the above reasons alone, it stands out as a masterwork. Yet the painting was not well received when it first appeared. According to Samuel van Hoogstraten, a student of Rembrandt's at the time: "Many people were of the opinion that, instead of presenting a series of individual portraits which he had been commissioned to do, the artist took his own wishes too much into consideration."[5]

Was *The Night Watch* a dismal failure that began the decline of the great artist's career? That has been debated. What is clear is that Rembrandt's decline was painful and tragic.

Dutch Masters

The phrase *Dutch Masters* has been used by a cigar company for one of its products. The term also refers to a group of masterly painters, including Rembrandt.

Dutch Masters are considered to be those from the Dutch Golden Age of Painting, which coincides with the Dutch Golden Age. This was a period when Dutch power and influence was at its height, and the painters known as Dutch Masters exerted a powerful influence on the world of art. They changed the way certain types of subjects were depicted.

Typical subjects for the Dutch Masters were historical events, portraits (both individual and group), landscapes, cityscapes, still lifes, and everyday occurrences. The paintings were often allegorical, meaning that certain objects were used to mean something else. An extinguished candle might signify the end of life.

With historical painting, which also included biblical scenes, the Dutch Masters rejected attempts to awe the audience, and instead substituted a realistic approach. Group portraits evolved from a static pose, such as people sitting at a table, to more dynamic scenes. Scientists might be shown holding instruments, while military captains might be pictured shouting orders to their troops.

Girl with a Pearl Earring, *known as the* Mona Lisa of the North, *Johannes Vermeer*

Landscapes, which had previously been depicted unrealistically and owed much to the artist's imagination, also changed under the Dutch Masters. Outdoor scenes were shown as they actually were, allowing the artists to realistically depict skies, seas, oceans, and fields.

Among the painters considered to be Dutch Masters are Rembrandt, Ferdinand Bol, Gerald Dou, Pieter de Hooch, Nicolas Maes, Paulus Potter, and Johannes Vermeer.

Balaam's Ass shows how Rembrandt gave biblical scenes a natural look and feel. The painting is also a fine example of the artist's use of color.

two

The Budding Artist

"Here is your child. May Our Lord grant you much happiness through him, else may He call him back to Him soon."[1] These are the words that midwives in Holland traditionally said upon the birth of a child. It is possible that they are the first words Rembrandt Harmenszoon van Rijn heard as he was put into the arms of his mother, Cornelia, on July 15, 1606.

Cornelia (or Neeltgen) Willemsdochter van Zuytbrouck was the daughter of a baker. Rembrandt's father, Harmen Gerritszoon van Rijn, was a miller. The baby was named after Remigia—his mother's grandmother. They lived in the city of Leiden in North Holland, a province in the Netherlands.

Harmen's family had come to Leiden around 1575, when they bought the windmill that overlooked a branch of the Rhine River called the Galgewater. (Rembrandt's last name, Van Rijn, means "from the Rhine.") Cornelia's family was well-to-do, and when Harmen married her he wanted her to keep her comfortable lifestyle. He bought a windmill from his family, part of an adjacent building, and a new house facing the windmill. It was in this home, on a street called Weddesteeg, that Rembrandt was likely born.

While there is disagreement over how many brothers and sisters Rembrandt had, many sources say he was the fifth son of seven children: four brothers and two sisters.[2] His brothers all pursued careers: Gerrit was a miller like his father, Adriaen a shoemaker, Willem a baker like his mother's father, and Cornelis an artisan. His sisters were Machteld and Lijsbeth. Women were not expected to have a trade in those days.

That Rembrandt or any baby born then survived infancy was fortunate. Medicine wasn't nearly as advanced as it is today, and beliefs were much different. Fresh air was considered harmful, so babies were wrapped in clothes and blankets like mummies and kept in rooms with no fresh air. Water did not often touch an infant's skin.

Rembrandt did survive, of course, and most likely played in the streets of Leiden. The town of 80,000 people was one of the most important in Holland and the second largest after Amsterdam. Although it was an industrial community, it contained the famous Leiden University, founded in 1575. One thing that Leiden was proud of was the cleanliness of its highways. The town, however, had no organized sewage system. Waste was usually dumped into nearby canals, fouling the water and creating a terrible smell.

Rembrandt's family life seems to have been filled with love and tolerance. His mother was devoted to the Bible, and in later years he painted her affectionately as she read from the book or prayed. At around age seven Rembrandt entered the Latin School in Leiden. He seems to have gotten a good education there, for his paintings display his knowledge of classical literature and other events. On May 20, 1620, when he was fourteen years old, he enrolled at Leiden University. Although his family may have wanted him to pursue a career like his brothers, there was apparently no objection to his going to school. Perhaps his artistic talent was already evident.

Rembrandt did not enjoy university life. The curriculum at Leiden included subjects such as law, theology, and medicine. None of these would help Rembrandt become an artist. After a few months, he left the school. What he needed was an apprenticeship to learn the technical points of art.

This was a fortunate time for aspiring artists in Holland. The country was becoming a strong economic force in Europe. People were prosperous and the market for portraits was booming. It is possible that Rembrandt's father knew this, and therefore let his son pursue art.[3]

The young artist was apprenticed to a local painter named Jacob Isaacsz van Swanenburgh, whom Rembrandt's parents knew. Rembrandt spent three years with Swanenburgh, but apparently the older man was a mediocre artist who could teach him only the basics of painting.[4]

Rembrandt was greatly influenced by the next artist he studied under, named Pieter Lastman. Sources disagree about how Rembrandt found out about Lastman. Some say that while he was studying under Swanenburgh he became friends with Jan Lievens, who had studied under Lastman and recommended him.[5] Others say that Rembrandt did not meet Lievens until after his time with Lastman.[6]

Rembrandt traveled to the Dutch city of Amsterdam in 1624 to study with Lastman. We assume that this period lasted only six months, because Lastman wrote a receipt for payment he was given after he "instructed Rembrandt, son of Harmen in the art of painting for half a year."[7]

Earlier in his career, Lastman had been to Italy, where he was greatly influenced by a growing movement to use light and shadow in a dramatic, realistic way. This was typified by the Italian artist Caravaggio.[8] Lastman was also the premier artist in Holland for the painting of religious and mythological subjects. His paintings had an almost lifelike look that made his work very popular. Lastman brought the Italian art world to Rembrandt. Rembrandt absorbed these lessons in the use of chiaroscuro (the interplay of light and shadow), realism, and the depiction of religious and mythological subjects. Like any great artist, Rembrandt did not just duplicate these lessons. He filtered and enhanced them until they became his own.

It is likely that Rembrandt was also influenced by the vibrant city of Amsterdam. The major city in the Netherlands, Amsterdam was a bustling port. Ships brought goods from throughout the known world. They also brought people of many races and ethnicities. Rembrandt, like any good artist, was a keen observer of people. They were, after all, his models.

After Lastman, he may have studied with a painter named Jacob Pynas in Amsterdam.[9] A plague outbreak in the city may have been the reason Rembrandt returned to Leiden.[10] In 1625, at the age of nineteen, he went back to the city of his birth to begin his career as an artist.

Upon his return to Leiden, Rembrandt and Jan Lievens renewed their friendship. Both were around the same age, interested in historical painting, and had studied under Lastman. The two set up a studio in Rembrandt's parents' house. Researchers differ on whether Rembrandt and Lievens worked together on any paintings. The two may have retouched and added other finishing details to each other's work since their styles were so similar.

Rembrandt was rapidly developing the techniques that would one day make him famous. These techniques were all on display in the painting

The Prophetess Anna, in which many historians believe Rembrandt's mother is portrayed. Rembrandt had great respect for the elderly, and liked nothing more than painting them because he felt that their faces would provide fresh insight to the human condition. His mother was one of his favorite subjects.

Balaam's Ass. This depiction of a biblical story shows Balaam about to strike the ass he is riding with a stick. Balaam's red clothing sharply contrasts the muted brown of the animal and surroundings. The white robes of the angel alongside Balaam seem to glow. The painting realistically depicts its subjects.

Another thing that clearly identified Rembrandt's paintings was his fondness and deep respect for age. The older people he drew seemed to have a wisdom and experience in their eyes and bearing that could only come from living for a long time. Rembrandt would always display the same care and understanding for his elderly subjects. It showed in paintings of his mother reading the Bible and of his father wearing Asian-style clothing.

Rembrandt was beginning to attract attention as an artist. In 1628 a man named Aernout van Buchell visited Leiden and wrote in his diary: "The Leiden miller's son is greatly praised, but before his time."[11]

Before long, it would not be premature to admire Rembrandt.

The Dutch Golden Age

The Netherlands, a small country in Europe, once enjoyed a period called the Dutch Golden Age. (The Netherlands is sometimes mistakenly called Holland. Two of the Netherlands's twelve provinces are called Holland—North Holland and South Holland.)

In the time before Rembrandt was born, the Netherlands was ruled by Spain. In 1568 war broke out between the two, as the Netherlands sought independence. By 1600 the northern part of the Netherlands was independent, but the south remained under Spanish control. The north was called the Dutch Republic, and included North Holland and South Holland. The Southern Netherlands, also called the Spanish Netherlands, included Flanders and Luxembourg. Trouble between the two sides brewed until 1648, when the Treaty of Munster forced Spain to give independence to all of the Netherlands.

Even before this the Dutch Republic had been growing into an economic power. Much of the seventeenth century is sometimes called the Dutch Golden Age. The movement was led by Amsterdam, which became one of the wealthiest cities in Europe. Amsterdam had the first full-time stock exchange in Europe. Because of its prosperity and religious tolerance, people poured into the city. Amsterdam's population jumped from 30,000 in 1565 to 130,000 by 1630. In the first half of the seventeenth century, the income of its citizens was the highest in Europe. Amsterdam's prosperity was so great that it became known as the Athens of the North.

The Netherlands also became a seagoing power. As early as 1600, ships returned from Asia with spices and other goods, and this sea trade expanded throughout the first half of the seventeenth century. Eventually the Dutch fleet numbered 16,000 ships. The power of their ships helped the Dutch launch a global empire that touched even the New World. New York City eventually became part of England's empire, but it was founded by the Dutch as New Amsterdam in the early 1600s.

The Netherlands faded into the background as England became the most dominant country in the world. But the confidence and wealth of the Netherlands during its Golden Age coincided with the years that Rembrandt was painting, quite possibly influencing him in his depictions of his subjects.

Dam Square, Amsterdam, *painted by Gerrit Adriaenszoon Berckheyde*

Self Portrait, 1628. Rembrandt produced dozens of self-portraits. They provide a photographic-type record of the changes in the artist as he traveled through life.

Making a Name for Himself

Around 1628 an energetic man entered the studio of Rembrandt and Lievens—a man who was to have an important impact on them. His name was Constantyn Huygens, and he was the secretary to the Prince of Orange.

Huygens was a player in the Leiden art scene, and his appearance at the studio of the two young painters showed that their reputation was growing. He was highly impressed by the two. In his biography, which he began writing about a year later, he lavishly praised the young painters. He thought they were as good as the most famous artists in the world, and they would soon be better.

Huygens was very impressed by one of Rembrandt's works called *Judas Returning the Thirty Pieces of Silver.* The painting depicted the biblical story of Judas returning the money he received for betraying Jesus to the authorities. Huygens said that the painting could be favorably compared with any produced in Italy, which at that time was considered to be the home of the greatest artists in the world. In a particularly revealing part of his text, Huygens noted that Rembrandt seemed to be superior in the vivid way he expressed his subjects' emotions, while Lievens was the more inventive.[1]

Huygens was also concerned for the health of Rembrandt and Lievens. He indicated that they did nothing but work at their art, denying themselves any of the typical pleasures of youth. Huygens suggested that they both go to Italy to study the works of famous artists such as Michelangelo. The young men did not follow his advice.

As Rembrandt's reputation continued to grow, two students came to study with him, providing a source of income. One of those was fourteen-year-old Gerrit Dou, who would go on to become another popular artist of his time.

A painting done soon after Dou's arrival likely provides a glimpse of the studio where Rembrandt and Lievens worked. It shows a room with wooden furniture and walls of crumbling plaster.

Around 1630 Rembrandt did some other work quite different from his usual biblical scenes and historical paintings. He made a series of etchings of beggars, nude women, and people urinating. What is most striking about them is the realistic way he depicted his subjects. While another artist may have tried to idealize these subjects, Rembrandt showed how they really looked.

Rembrandt was known as much for his etchings as he was for his paintings.[2] He was one of the first to use etchings to make prints of his portraits and scatter them throughout the city as advertisements for himself and his work.

Events were moving swiftly for the young artist. In April 1630 his father died. Because of Huygens, Rembrandt was beginning to receive commissions for his work. Rembrandt established a business relationship with an art dealer in Amsterdam named Hendrik van Uylenburgh. Around the end of 1630, Lievens left Leiden for England.

Quite likely all of these factors came together for Rembrandt in his decision to leave Leiden for Amsterdam. Compared to wealthy Amsterdam, Leiden was just a small university town with limited opportunities. In the spring of 1631, the young artist moved to Amsterdam. He would spend the rest of his life there.

Rembrandt arrived in Amsterdam accompanied by his sister Lijsbeth, whom he had often sketched and painted. The artist moved into van Uylenburgh's house. Soon he received an important commission and painted what many consider to be his first masterpiece: *The Anatomy Lesson of Dr. Nicolaes Tulp.*

Tulp was one of Amsterdam's top physicians. The custom in the city at the time was to portray people at group functions. In the picture, Tulp is shown dissecting the corpse of an armed robber named Aris Kindt in the anatomy theater of the Amsterdam Guild of Surgeons. Tulp and the corpse are surrounded by a group of onlookers. (Dissections had only recently been authorized in Holland and could only be performed on criminals, so a dissection was a major event.)

The problem that artists faced with group pictures was that they were required to provide accurate portraits of every person in attendance. Often artists showed everyone staring straight ahead, which gave the picture a stilted, staged feeling.

Rembrandt solved this problem by grouping Dr. Tulp's students around the corpse. They are all focused on a key moment in the action: Tulp has just removed the skin of an arm and is lifting the limb by an instrument, showing its muscle structure. By having the corpse almost completely illuminated (except for a small part of the face), Rembrandt makes the body the center of attention—the thing to which the eye is first drawn. Then the eye goes to the figure of Dr. Tulp. The last thing that draws attention is the group of students, crowding in to see what the doctor is doing. The corpse is bathed in a greenish light, while the living subjects are shown in natural light. All of the elements in the picture—the grouping of subjects, the lighting, the way objects are depicted—mark it as a brilliant painting. If Rembrandt's intention in moving to Amsterdam was to receive commissions and make money, *The Anatomy Lesson of Dr. Nicolaes Tulp* was a fabulous calling card for the young artist. All Amsterdam recognized the picture as something special, and soon Rembrandt was buried by commissions.

Most of the commissions were for portraits. Of fifty paintings he did in 1632 and 1633, all but four are portraits.[3] Amsterdam society was at the height of its power. Confident men and women with money to spend sought out the young painter so that he could immortalize them on canvas.

Along the way Rembrandt became wealthy. Suddenly he had more than enough money, and he didn't hesitate to spend it. As he was described in this period of wealth: "He often went to public sales by auction; and here he acquired clothes that were old-fashioned and disused as long as they struck him as bizarre and picturesque, and those, even though at times they were downright dirty, he hung on the walls of his studio."[4]

At these auctions Rembrandt would acquire other items—arrows, daggers, knives, helmets, and works of art—that he fancied. He would bid so high at auctions that no one bothered to try to top him.

Rembrandt made many important friends while he was living in van Ulyenburgh's house, because they were both involved in art and attracted people who were interested in art. The most important person that Rembrandt met there was the woman who would become his wife.

Twenty-year-old Saskia van Ulyenburgh was the daughter of Rombert van Ulyenburgh, the burgomaster (mayor) of the town of Friesland. He had died when she was twelve, and the girl had come to Amsterdam to live with her uncle. The romance between Rembrandt and Saskia was not approved of by most of her family.[5] She was the wealthy daughter of an important town official, while he was a miller's son. Van Ulyenburgh did support them, however, and the couple got engaged in June 1633. To celebrate, Rembrandt made a silverpoint etching of Saskia. Silverpoint is a difficult medium that allows no mistakes. A thin silver stylus is used to draw on expensive white vellum paper. Rembrandt carefully chose it to commemorate the event. Beneath the sketch, in Rembrandt's handwriting, are the words: "This is drawn after my wife, when she was 21 years old, the third day after our betrothal—the 8th of June, 1633."[6] (Other sources list the date as June 18.[7])

On June 22, 1634, the two were married in the Reformed Church of Sint-Annaparochie. Rembrandt's mother was still alive. She was required to give her consent to the nuptials, which she did at the notary public in Leiden. It is also possible that she attended the wedding and the lavish ceremony that followed. Although there is no specific record of Rembrandt's celebration, at the time it was customary for at least twenty courses of food to be served to guests.[8]

After the wedding Rembrandt and Saskia lived in van Ulyenburgh's house. Saskia was a frequent subject of Rembrandt's art. Using the clothes and other props he had purchased, Rembrandt put his new wife in a variety of poses and settings, including as the goddess Flora with a crown of flowers. Rembrandt biographer Charles Fowkes said: "In all the portraits he invites us to look up to her, admire her, stand in awe of her—just as he does."[9]

Saskia as Flora, 1635. Rembrandt loved to dress his wife, Saskia, in costumes and portray her in a variety of poses. She modeled as Flora, the goddess of flowers, in several of his paintings. To the artist, there was no greater beauty than his wife.

One portrait of the couple at this time shows the happiness that Rembrandt felt. In *The Prodigal Son in the Tavern (Rembrandt and Saskia)*, he is dressed like a musketeer, complete with feathered hat and sword. Saskia is sitting on his lap, looking over her shoulder, and smiling. In one hand, a grinning Rembrandt holds a tall glass of beer as if giving a toast. His other hand is wrapped lightly around Saskia's waist. They seem confident and carefree.

The Prodigal Son in the Tavern shows Rembrandt and Saskia in the early, carefree days of their marriage. Life was good; they were young, they had plenty of money, and the future looked bright. But soon things would change.

Rembrandt could afford to be happy. He was making good money as an artist, and marriage to Saskia had brought him more money and increased social standing. He was a young artist in demand, and the future seemed bright.

Little did Rembrandt realize the troubles that were about to befall him.

The Other Side of Prosperity

During Rembrandt's time, the Netherlands was considered the richest and most prosperous country in the world. Prosperity for some does not mean prosperity for all, and there were many people at the time who did not share in the wealth.

The lower-class citizens in the Netherlands were not as fortunate as the upper classes. The peasants and laborers were forced to contend with poverty and hardship in a manner similar to that which existed in England nearly a century later, at the start of the Industrial Revolution. For instance, Leiden, Rembrandt's birthplace, contained an estimated 20,000 textile mill workers.[10] Almost all of these people lived in tiny huts where the main furnishing was straw.

Government officials were not blind to these conditions. Amsterdam leaders ordered that bakers of fancy cakes should not overdecorate these cakes and then place them in shop windows. Officials were worried that the sight of such delicious desserts might sadden poor people who could not afford them.

Children fared little better in this society that loved to celebrate itself through portraits. They were plucked from alongside highways in Germany

and other countries, and from out of orphanages, and put to work in the textile mills. It is estimated that one businessman in Leiden alone "imported" 4,000 of these children over a ten-year period.

In 1644 the authorities finally took action on behalf of working children throughout the country: They decreed that no child should have to work more than fourteen hours per day.

This was the reality of life for those less fortunate than others.

Poor boy looking in window

Self-Portrait, 1658. As Rembrandt aged, his face revealed the many troubles he had encountered throughout his life. By 1658 he had endured the death of his wife, commercial indifference to his art, and financial problems.

four

Tragic Fame

Rembrandt enjoyed dressing himself and his wife in fancy costumes. He wanted to be seen as a man of substance, and as a proper husband for Saskia. It is also possible that he was seeking a change of pace from the austere portraits of black-clothed subjects that he was constantly painting. By putting himself and his wife in outrageous clothes and settings, he was able to free his keen imagination and creativity.[1]

Rembrandt produced a hundred self-portraits throughout his life.[2] He left no autobiographical writings, but his self-portraits help us understand how he felt and how he looked as he aged. He used art to show people's feelings. His self-portraits help us understand the man and the artist at various points of his life.

Most of his pictures of Saskia were painted from 1632 to 1634. After that they became fewer, and in some years he did none. That's probably because tragedy began stalking the young couple.

It started with their children. In December 1635 Saskia gave birth to the couple's first child, a boy they named Rumbartus, after her father. The baby lived only two months. In July 1638 the couple had a girl, whom they called Cornelia. She did not live more than a few weeks.

These deaths had a devastating effect on Saskia. Rembrandt ruthlessly records the unpleasant events in his personal life, primarily via line drawing or wash, the artistic mediums that he often used when expressing his innermost thoughts. In one heartbreaking drawing, baby Rumbartus lies near death, his eyes closed and his small body in distress. Most of the drawings depict the deterioration of Saskia. She passes from a carefree young girl to a tired-looking housewife to a sick, bedridden woman as clearly as if she had been photographed instead of drawn.

During these years the couple moved several times. They rented until 1639, when Rembrandt bought a large three-story house in the Breestraat section of Amsterdam. This and his other purchases—paintings by other artists, Japanese fans, porcelain from China, and whatever else struck his fancy—severely strained the artist's finances. Some researchers have concluded that Saskia was a bad influence on Rembrandt, encouraging him in his life of reckless spending.[3]

Rembrandt hated being considered a wasteful spender. It particularly incensed him when people said that his wild spending was draining his wife's dowry. In 1638 he filed a slander suit against people he said were spreading tales about him wasting Saskia's money. The suit was dismissed.

Rembrandt had continued to receive important commissions during this time, many coming from Constanyn Huygens. In the early 1630s he received one from Huygens for a series of five paintings showing different biblical scenes from the trial and execution of Jesus (the Passion). The paintings were intended for Frederick Henry, Prince of Orange. The prince was furnishing several homes, and it is believed that the paintings were for one of them, Noordeinde Palace.

Rembrandt's association with Huygens had proved to be very important in terms of profit and prestige. This time Huygens not only got Rembrandt work, he supervised it. The problems that developed between the two ended their relationship.

Huygens and the prince greatly admired the work of Flemish artist Peter Paul Rubens, who was in the twilight of his brilliant career. It seems that Huygens, having convinced the prince to use Rembrandt, wanted the Passion paintings to imitate Rubens's style. Rembrandt was no mimic and he refused.

Rembrandt's *Descent from the Cross* shows the body of Jesus being taken down from the cross. It shows the throng of mourners surrounding the body and other background details. This was in contrast to Rubens's more dramatic style, which zeroed in on the central action. Perhaps the biggest change in the paintings came in Rembrandt's depiction of the figures. He did

The Descent From the Cross, illustrates the realistic manner in which Rembrandt portrayed Biblical subjects. The body of Jesus is depicted as limp and sagging — certainly not beautiful as other artists may have shown it.

not beautify them, but rather portrayed them with an intense realism. In *Descent* there is nothing beautiful about the body of Christ. It sags down, the head lolling to one side, looking like any corpse would. It is a limp, pathetic figure—hardly glorious.

Another thing that Rembrandt did was insert himself in some of his paintings. In *Descent* he is standing on a ladder helping to lower Jesus' body; in *Elevation,* another painting in the series, he is a soldier who tries to push the cross into an upright position. His point was that all humanity shares in the guilt for the Crucifixion.[4]

The Passion paintings prompted a series of seven letters from Rembrandt to Huygens. This is all of the artist's correspondence that has survived. Because of this, art historians and Rembrandt's biographers have scoured these letters for clues as to what type of man he was. The letters are primarily pleas from Rembrandt for more money than he received for the Passion paintings, along with defenses of the work.

The rift that opened between Rembrandt and Huygens was significant, because the Passion paintings marked the end of their association. Huygens was even reluctant to accept a painting Rembrandt offered as a gift called *The Blinding of Samson*. Rembrandt sent it anyway.

The Blinding of Samson, painted in 1636, is Rembrandt's most violent work. It shows Philistine soldiers rushing into a tent and plunging a dagger into the eye of Samson as he contorts in agony. Delilah is shown holding Samson's cut-off hair and fleeing from the scene with a half-gloating, half-sympathetic look on her face as she watches what is happening to him. She is a figure both terrifying and pathetic. Again Rembrandt employs light and shadow effectively, as the scene with Samson is illuminated only by the light let into the tent by the opening through which Delilah is escaping.

Rembrandt took on a large mortgage to pay for the new house he and Saskia bought in 1639. It was next door to van Ulyenburgh's house. Along with his continued passion for collecting, the mortgage drained money from him. To increase his income, Rembrandt took on greater numbers of pupils. One estimate is that at least fifty known Dutch artists were his students at some point.[5]

If Rembrandt hoped that the move into a new house would change his and Saskia's luck, he was disappointed. In July 1640 the couple's second daughter, also named Cornelia, was born, but she died a few weeks later. Saskia deteriorated further. In September 1640 the artist's mother died.

In the spring of 1641, Saskia was again expecting a child. Rembrandt's son Titus was born in September 1641 and survived. This time it was not the child who died. It was Saskia who would not survive. She grew progressively weaker throughout the winter and died on June 14, 1642. She was not even thirty years old.

The Blinding of Samson is another one of Rembrandt's works based on a biblical story. In an earlier painting in 1628 the artist had portrayed the same subject just before the attack, leaving it to the imagination to realize what was going to happen. Here, however, the entire scene is shown in its horrible cruelty.

In the year of his greatest personal tragedy, Rembrandt produced what many consider his greatest painting, *The Night Watch*. Captain Cocq was pleased with the result, since he is featured in the foreground of the portrait. The painting was hung prominently in the unit's headquarters.

Other members of the group were not pleased. They had paid to be in a group portrait, only to appear in half-shadow, with their faces partially obscured. While Rembrandt's biographers debate about whether the portrait

Belshazzar's Feast illustrates Rembrandt's continuing interest in biblical subjects. He depicts the exact moment when a divine message appears on the wall, forecasting the imminent end of the rule of the King of Babylon.

was a success or failure, writer Joseph-Emile Muller makes two interesting points. One is that revolutionary works of art are often imitated, yet no one copied the style of *The Night Watch*.[6] The other is that Rembrandt was not asked to do another group portrait for fourteen years.[7]

In her will, Saskia left her half of the estate to Titus, but allowed Rembrandt to use it until the boy came of age. She added a stipulation that if Rembrandt remarried, her estate portion should go to her sister Hiskje. In 1643 Rembrandt painted Saskia one last time, returning her to the beautiful young woman she had been when they were first married.

To help him take care of little Titus and run the house while he painted and taught his students, Rembrandt hired a woman named Geertghe Direx. She was the widow of a trumpet player named Abraham Claesz. Unfortunately, the song she was to play for Rembrandt was a sad one.

Peter Paul Rubens

Although many consider Rembrandt to be the world's greatest artist, others would argue that an even more important artist who lived at almost the same time was the Flemish genius Peter Paul Rubens.

Peter Paul Rubens was born in Siegen, Westphalia (which is today part of Germany), on June 28, 1577. His family was originally from Flanders. Rubens's father, Jan, had converted his religion from Catholicism to Calvinism, a Protestant religion, and was forced to flee Flanders in 1568 when violence broke out there against Protestants.

After Jan Rubens's death in 1587, his widow and family returned to Antwerp, Flanders, where they became Catholics. Peter Paul Rubens was an exceptional student. He could speak six different languages. Like Rembrandt, his artistic genius was recognized early. At just twenty-one years old, he was given the rank of master painter of the Antwerp Guild of Saint Luke. In 1600, Rubens went to Italy, which at the time was the center of the art world. There he became employed as an artist by the duke of the Italian state of Mantua. He also became a diplomat and took on occasional missions for the duke.

It was after he returned to Antwerp in 1608 that his reputation as an artist became legendary. Rubens developed a painting style that combined great color and shimmering light with exceptional energy. His paintings seemed to vibrate with action. He also became a master at

Descent from the Cross, *by Peter Paul Rubens*

portraying biblical scenes, and was greatly in demand as a painter. Rubens became so busy that he had an enormous workshop filled with paintings under development. He would sketch out the initial scene and images, and then add the final touches, leaving it to his assistants to create the bulk of the work.

Rubens grew so rich from his work that he built a gigantic home in Antwerp in the ornate style of an Italian palace. He also remained busy with his diplomatic work, and performed missions to Paris, Spain, and England. He died on May 30, 1640.

Titus in a Monk Habit, painted in 1660. Titus, Rembrandt and Saskia's son, was a frequent subject of Rembrandt's paintings.

five

Bitter Years

After Saskia's death Rembrandt began painting landscapes, a subject he had previously ignored. He largely abandoned the theatrical themes he had once favored for the simpler ones of nature. He also began using Amsterdam's large Jewish population, as well as his son Titus, as models for figures in his paintings.[1]

There is the possibility that he lived in England for a period in 1661, but the truth of this account is unknown.[2] This uncertainty plagues most of what we know of Rembrandt's life. Little is actually known about him. He apparently did not like interruptions when he worked, and he could be very defensive about his art.[3] He painted a portrait of a Portuguese merchant, who did not like the finished product. When the merchant expressed his opinion to Rembrandt, the artist told him that his opinion didn't matter.[4]

It also seems that Rembrandt could be vindictive. After Geertghe Direx had been employed by Rembrandt as his infant son's nurse, she possibly became his lover. It must have been extremely difficult for Direx to compete with the idealized images of Saskia that were all about. Then, in the mid-1640s, a woman named Hendrickje Stoffels also entered the artist's household. She eventually became Rembrandt's wife in every way but name. (It is an indication of how little information is available about Rembrandt that some sources mention only Direx[5] and others mention only Stoffels.[6])

Around 1648, Direx left Rembrandt's employ. Shortly after that she sued the artist for breach of promise, claiming that he said he'd marry her and never followed through.

The Mill, c.1650. In his later years Rembrandt painted more landscapes. Although his subjects had changed, Rembrandt still brought his masterly use of light and shadow to landscape paintings.

For Rembrandt to have made such a promise would have been costly. Under the terms of Saskia's will, if he remarried he would have lost the use of her income. Nevertheless, when Direx produced a ring that she claimed Rembrandt had given her as a sign of his intentions, the court ruled in her favor. Rembrandt was ordered to pay her a yearly amount of money at a time when he could hardly afford it.

The artist's vindictive streak emerged when Direx got into debt and had to pawn some of Saskia's jewels that Rembrandt had given her. Furious with her and still angry about the court decision, Rembrandt paid a notary to take sworn statements from people saying that Direx was promiscuous. He then brought this information to the court, and succeeded in having Direx committed for twelve years to a reformatory for people of questionable character. She languished there for five years until she was released, most likely because of illness. Within eighteen months she was dead.

Because he was living with Stoffels without being married to her, Rembrandt lost the goodwill (and almost certainly commissions) of Amsterdam's art patrons. In 1648 he made a sketch of himself. Far from the carefree youth of the early days, the sketch depicts a weary man who has experienced misfortune and sadness.

As the artist entered the 1650s, more unhappiness was to befall him. Stoffels and Rembrandt had a son, but he died on August 15, 1652. In 1654 they were expecting another child. However, their relationship had caused much concern in Amsterdam's society. Three times that year she was called before the Council of the Reformed Church to defend her life with Rembrandt. All three times she refused to show up, but she decided to answer a fourth summons. At that appearance the record stated that Stoffels "confesses to [breaking church law] with Rembrandt the painter."[7] As a punishment she was forbidden from taking Holy Communion. On October 30 a daughter was born to the couple. Rembrandt named the child Cornelia.

His shaky finances were fast falling apart. In the 1650s Rembrandt was often borrowing money. He took loans from friends twice in 1653. Both times he promised to pay back the money in one year, and offered all his belongings as security. He still owed a considerable amount on his large house. He scrambled to collect money that he felt was owed him, but it was far too little.

One thing that hurt Rembrandt financially was his insistence on following his artistic heart, no matter where it might lead, such as with *The Night Watch*. In one instance, a friend named Jan Six wrote a poem called *Medea,* and asked Rembrandt to produce a drawing for it. The drawing that Rembrandt made had nothing to do with the poem.

Another problem was simply the number of Rembrandt's students. Many of them took from Rembrandt the qualities the public had once liked in his art, while rejecting other, more personal choices. It was possible for people to seek out Rembrandt-like work from his students rather than going to the master himself.

On May 17, 1656, Rembrandt transferred the deed to his house to fourteen-year-old Titus in order to save it from being snatched up by creditors. The maneuver caused the artist's many creditors to panic, and they pushed Rembrandt even harder for the money he owed them. He responded by having the Amsterdam town council declare him bankrupt.

On July 25 and 26, 1656, an inventory was made of Rembrandt's possessions so that they could be sold and the money paid to his creditors. The list of items was staggering, and showed that Rembrandt was an enthusiastic collector of anything and everything. The list included paintings, sculptures, medals, glasses, robes, coral, shells, helmets, musical instruments, chairs, crossbows—in short, enough material to staff the prop department of a modern theater company.

After 1650 the prosperity of the Dutch citizens declined, as England began asserting itself as a major power and challenging Dutch supremacy on the seas. Rembrandt's possessions did not fetch as much at auction as they might have ten years earlier. To add insult to injury, he was forced to take a room at an inn called Keizerkroon and watch as his precious treasures were slowly sold.

Finally the house and its furnishings were bought, with the house bringing less than what he had paid for it. On December 18, 1660, Rembrandt closed the door for the last time on the home he had bought for Saskia, when the world seemed full of promise. He, Stoffels, Titus, and baby Cornelia moved to a small, simple house in a section of Amsterdam called Jordan.

If people thought Rembrandt was broken by recent events, they were mistaken. An artist who had studied under Rembrandt was commissioned for a painting to hang inside the new Amsterdam Town Hall. When the artist died suddenly, the authorities asked Rembrandt to do the painting instead. His *Conspiracy of Julius Civilis* was not a noble painting glorifying freedom fighters in ancient Rome, but a study in evil. All of the characters look immoral, and the one-eyed Julius is terrifying. A sickly yellow-green light adds to the sense of foreboding. The picture was briefly hung in the town hall, then taken down and replaced.

In the final years of his life, Rembrandt was comforted by the presence of Stoffels. She was a loving companion and remained with him even when

The Conspiracy of Julius Civilis was not well received.

they lost all their possessions and were forced to move. She formed a company with Titus in December 1660 to help sell Rembrandt's paintings and shield him from his creditors, who were still owed money. On October 27, 1662, Rembrandt was even forced to sell the family tomb—the place where Saskia was buried. It seems likely that Stoffels, who had been ill for some time, had died around then. Quite possibly Rembrandt sold one tomb in order to afford another.

Fate had one final shock for the old artist. In February 1668 Titus married a woman named Magdalena. Seven months later, with Magdalena expecting their child, Titus died. Magdalena gave birth to a daughter, whom she named Titia in honor of her husband. Rembrandt attended the child's baptism on March 22, 1669. His strength rapidly fading, Rembrandt returned to the Bible for one of his last paintings, *The Return of the Prodigal Son.* The painting carries an optimistic message—the spiritual homecoming of all humanity—and indicates that Rembrandt still felt hope.

On October 4, 1669, at the age of sixty-three, Rembrandt died. Although his brush had been stilled, Rembrandt left behind a marvelous collection of work. Centuries after his death, people are still finding new things in his art to admire, argue over, and reflect upon.

The Return of the Prodigal Son is considered by some to be one of Rembrandt's greatest works. It was painted near the end of his life, but its message of hope showed that the artist was still optimistic.

Master of Light

What is it that makes Rembrandt's paintings great? Why is his name remembered while those of countless other artists have been swallowed by time?

There are many qualities that make Rembrandt's art memorable. Great art functions on many levels, and there are certainly numerous things to admire in Rembrandt's work, such as his choice and grouping of subjects and his use of color. Perhaps the most important thing to notice about Rembrandt's work is his use of light and shadow.

The affluent Dutch had an unquenchable thirst for having their portraits painted. It was their way of announcing their success. They wanted the paintings created their way. For an individual portrait, the picture had to be somber and businesslike—in short, an accurate representation of a serious businessman, even if it was dull and lifeless. Group portraits had to give each member of the group equal importance.

What was an artist to do when faced with these restrictions on his creativity? Some artists just did as their subjects asked. Others found a way around these limits. For Rembrandt, the way around was through light. Rembrandt made light an active force in his work, instead of just a static object. By illuminating a portion of his work with a particular light—such as the greenish glow on the corpse in *Dr. Tulp*—Rembrandt skillfully draws the eye toward that spot.

Portrait of Jan Six

He also used light to simulate movement, such as in *Night Watch.* The figure bathed in white light in the middle of the portrait seems ready to step off the canvas. In *The Blinding of Samson,* the flash of light let in by the open tent flap shows Delilah sneaking out of the scene, her face a mixture of triumph and tragedy.

Rembrandt's masterful use of light is brilliant. It is one of many things that make him a great artist.

1606 Rembrandt Harmenszoon van Rijn is born.

1613 Rembrandt attends Latin School.

1620 He attends Leiden University, but drops out after a short time.

1624 The artist studies under Pieter Lastman in Amsterdam.

1625 He returns to his hometown of Leiden, and begins his artistic career.

1628 Rembrandt meets Constantyn Huygens.

1630 His father dies.

1631 He moves to Amsterdam.

1634 Rembrandt marries Saskia.

1635 Their son Rumbartus is born, but he dies in infancy.

1638 Their daughter Cornelia is born but dies.

1639 Rembrandt buys a large house that drains his finances.

1640 Saskia and Rembrandt have another daughter, also named Cornelia, who also dies.

1641 The couple's son Titus is born.

1642 Rembrandt's wife, Saskia, dies.

Mid-1640s Hendrickje Stoffels moves into the house and becomes Rembrandt's companion.

1652 Their newborn son dies.

1654 Their daughter, Cornelia, is born.

1656 Rembrandt declares bankruptcy.

1660 Rembrandt and Stoffels move to a smaller house along with Titus and Cornelia.

1662 Stoffels dies.

1669 Rembrandt's son Titus dies.

1669 Rembrandt dies.

1541	John Calvin establishes a new branch of Christianity; it will come to be called Calvinism.
1547	British King Henry VIII dies.
1558	Queen Elizabeth ascends the English throne.
1568	Dutch begin revolt against Spain.
1575	Leiden University is founded; it is a gift of William of Orange to the citizens of Leiden.
1582	The Gregorian calendar is instituted.
1584	Sir Walter Raleigh and his English expedition reach a landmass in the New World and name it Virginia in honor of the Virgin Queen Elizabeth.
1587	John White is named governor of the British colony at Roanoke Island in the New World.
1588	The British Navy defeats the Spanish Armada.
1600	The northern part of the Netherlands becomes independent of Spain.
1602	The Dutch East India Company is founded to establish trade routes to Asia and claim uncharted lands.
1603	Samuel de Champlain makes his first voyage from France to eastern Canada.
1607	The British establish Jamestown Colony in Virginia.
1608	Champlain founds Québec, which will become the French capital in North America.
1618	The Thirty Years' War begins in Europe.
1619	The first African slaves are brought to Virginia.
1620	The *Mayflower* lands in Plymouth.
1624	The first Dutch settlers arrive in New Netherland.
1648	The southern part of the Netherlands becomes independent of Spain.
1652	The First Anglo-Dutch War begins.
1665	The Great Plague strikes London.
1667	John Milton writes *Paradise Lost.*
1674	After the Third Anglo-Dutch War, New Netherland becomes New York.
1682	Peter I becomes czar of Russia.
1685	One of the last great—but unsuccessful—buccaneering raids is attempted on the city of Panama by a force of about 3,000 men led by Edward Davis and others.
1692	The Salem witch trials are held in Massachusetts.
1699	William Kidd is arrested for piracy in New York.
1745	Pieter van Musschenbroek invents the Leyden jar, a device that can store electrical charge, in Rembrandt's hometown.

1626	Balaam's Ass
c. 1628	Self Portrait, 1628
1629	Judas Returning the Thirty Pieces of Silver
1631	The Prophetess Anna
1632	The Anatomy Lesson of Dr. Nicolaes Tulp
c. 1633	Descent from the Cross
1634	Saskia as Flora
1635	Saskia as Flora
c. 1635	Belshazzar's Feast
c. 1635	The Prodigal Son in the Tavern (Rembrandt and Saskia)
1636	The Blinding of Samson
1642	The Company of Captain Frans Banning Cocq and Lieutenant Willem van Ruytenburgh (The Night Watch)
1648	Supper at Emmaus
c. 1650	The Mill
1653	Aristotle Contemplating a Bust of Homer
1654	Portrait of Jan Six
1655	Joseph Accused by Potiphar's Wife
1658	Self-Portrait, 1658
1660	Titus in a Monk Habit
1662	The Syndics of the Clothmaker's Guild (The Staalmeesters)
c. 1662	Conspiracy of Julius Civilis
1669	The Return of the Prodigal Son

Chapter One. The Masterpiece

1. Charles Fowkes. *The Life of Rembrandt* (London, England: The Hamlyn Publishing Group Limited, 1978), p. 21.
2. Robert Wallace. *The World of Rembrandt* (New York: Time-Life Books, 1968), p. 72.
3. Fowkes, p. 79.
4. Roger Housden. *How Rembrandt Reveals Your Beautiful, Imperfect Self* (New York: Harmony Books, 2005), p. 108.
5. Joseph-Emile Muller. *Rembrandt* (New York: Harry N. Abrams, Inc., 1969), p. 126.

Chapter Two. The Budding Artist

1. Charles Fowkes. *The Life of Rembrandt* (London, England: The Hamlyn Publishing Group Limited, 1978), p. 15.
2. Mario Lepore. *The Life, Times and Art of Rembrandt* (New York: Crescent Books, 1967), p. 4.
3. Fowkes, p. 22.
4. Joseph-Emile Muller. *Rembrandt* (New York: Harry N. Abrams, Inc., 1969), p. 8.
5. Lepore, p. 11.
6. Muller, p. 10.
7. Lepore, p. 12.
8. Roger Housden. *How Rembrandt Reveals Your Beautiful, Imperfect Self* (New York: Harmony Books, 2005), p. 18.
9. Muller, p. 10.
10. Lepore, p. 12.
11. Fowkes, p. 32.

Chapter Three. Making a Name for Himself

1. Joseph-Emile Muller. *Rembrandt* (New York: Harry N. Abrams, Inc., 1969), p. 11.
2. Roger Housden. *How Rembrandt Reveals Your Beautiful, Imperfect Self* (New York: Harmony Books, 2005), p. 22.
3. Charles Fowkes. *The Life of Rembrandt* (London, England: The Hamlyn Publishing Group Limited, 1978), p. 46.
4. Jakob Rosenberg. *Rembrandt* (London, England: Phaidon Press Limited, 1964), p. 22.

5. Mario Lepore. *The Life, Times and Art of Rembrandt* (New York: Crescent Books, 1967), p. 24.
6. Fowkes, p. 49.
7. Lepore, p. 24.
8. Fowkes, p. 56.
9. Ibid, p. 57.
10. Robert Wallace. *The World of Rembrandt* (New York: Time-Life Books, 1968), p. 92.

Chapter Four. Tragic Fame

1. Joseph-Emile Muller. *Rembrandt* (New York: Harry N. Abrams, Inc., 1969), p. 65.
2. Roger Housden. *How Rembrandt Reveals Your Beautiful, Imperfect Self* (New York: Harmony Books, 2005), p. 12.
3. Jakob Rosenberg. *Rembrandt* (London, England: Phaidon Press Limited, 1964), p. 23.
4. Robert Wallace. *The World of Rembrandt* (New York: Time-Life Books, 1968), p. 67.
5. Charles Fowkes. *The Life of Rembrandt* (London, England: The Hamlyn Publishing Group Limited, 1978), p. 74.
6. Muller, p. 127.
7. Ibid, p. 128.

Chapter Five. Bitter Years

1. Jakob Rosenberg. *Rembrandt* (London, England: Phaidon Press Limited, 1964), p. 26.
2. Charles Fowkes. *The Life of Rembrandt* (London, England: The Hamlyn Publishing Group Limited, 1978), p. 86.
3. Robert Wallace. *The World of Rembrandt* (New York: Time-Life Books, 1968), p. 93.
4. Ibid, p. 94.
5. Fowkes, p. 88.
6. Mario Lepore. *The Life, Times and Art of Rembrandt* (New York: Crescent Books, 1967), p. 53.
7. Fowkes, p. 112.

Books

de Bie, Ceciel, and Martijn Leenen. *Rembrandt: See and Do Children's Book.* Los Angeles: Getty Trust Publications, 2001.

Muhlberger, Richard. *What Makes a Rembrandt a Rembrandt?* New York: Viking Juvenile, 2002.

Niz, Xavier W. *Rembrandt.* Mankato, Minnesota: Bridgestone Books, 2004.

Pescio, Claudio, Sergio Ricciardi, and Andrea Ricciardi. *Rembrandt and 17th-Century Holland: The Dutch Nation and Its Painters.* New York: Peter Bedrick, 2001.

Works Consulted

Fowkes, Charles. *The Life of Rembrandt.* London, England: The Hamlyn Publishing Group Limited, 1978.

Housden, Roger. *How Rembrandt Reveals Your Beautiful, Imperfect Self.* New York: Harmony Books, 2005.

Kitson, Michael. *Rembrandt.* London, England: Phaidon Press Ltd, 1969.

Lepore, Mario. *The Life, Times and Art of Rembrandt.* New York: Crescent Books, 1967.

Muller, Joseph-Emile, *Rembrandt.* New York: Harry N. Abrams, Inc., 1969.

Roffo, Stefano, ed. *Rembrandt.* New York: Gramercy Books, 1994.

Rosenberg, Jakob. *Rembrandt.* London, England: Phaidon Press Limited, 1964.

Schama, Simon. *Rembrandt's Eyes.* New York: Alfred A. Knopf, 1999.

Schwartz, Gary. *Rembrandt.* New York: Viking Penguin, 1985.

Wallace, Robert. *The World of Rembrandt.* New York: Time-Life Books, 1968.

On the Internet

Artcyclopedia: Rembrandt van Rijn
  http://www.artcyclopedia.com/artists/rembrandt_van_rijn.html

Janson, Jonathan. *Rembrandt: Life, Paintings, Etchings, Drawings & Self Portraits,* 2005–2006.
  http://www.rembrandtpainting.net/

Olga's Gallery: Rembrandt Harmenszoon van Rijn
  http://www.abcgallery.com/R/rembrandt/rembrandt.html

Pioch, Nicolas. WebMuseum, Paris: Rembrandt, September 19, 2002
  http://www.ibiblio.org/wm/paint/auth/rembrandt/

Rembrandt House
  http://www.rembrandthuis.nl/cms_pages/index_main.html

apprenticeship (uh-PREN-tis-ship)—Time spent as a student learning a trade from an expert.

austere (aw-STEER)—Very simple; plain.

betrothal (bee-TROH-thul)—A promise to marry; engagement.

chiaroscuro (kee-ar-uh-SKYOOR-oh)—The interplay of light and shadow in a painting.

commemorate (kuh-MEH-muh-rayt)—To honor someone's memory.

coyly (KOY-lee)—Shyly.

Crucifixion (kroo-sih-FIK-shun)—The execution of Jesus, accomplished by nailing his hands and feet to a cross and leaving him to die.

curriculum (kuh-RIK-yoo-lum)—The course of study at a school.

deterioration (dee-teer-ee-or-AY-shun)—The process of breaking down.

enhanced (en-HANTST)—Added detail.

eroded (ee-ROH-ded)—Wore away.

etchings (ET-chingz)—Prints made from etched metal plates.

idealize (eye-DEEL-yz)—To make something seem better than it is.

immortalize (im-MOR-tal-yz)—To make someone's memory live forever.

incensed (in-SENTZD)—Inflamed with anger.

lavish (LAA-vish)—To use or give in great amounts.

nuptials (NUP-chulz)—Marriage; wedding.

pinnacle (PIH-nah-kul)—The highest point.

promiscuous (proh-MISS-kew-us)—Having many lovers.

rift (RIFT)—A break.

techniques (tek-NEEKS)—The ways ones skills are used to do something.

vindictive (vin-DIK-tiv)—Having the desire for revenge; spiteful.

INDEX